THE ANGEL OF HISTORY

THE ANGEL OF

HISTORY

—

Carolyn Forché

HarperCollins*Publishers*

HarperCollins books may be purchased for educational, business, or sales promotional use. For information please write: Special Markets Department, HarperCollins Publishers, Inc., 10 East 53rd Street, New York, NY 10022.

FIRST EDITION

Designed by Jessica Shatan

Library of Congress Cataloging-in Publication Data
Forché, Carolyn.
  The angel of history / Carolyn Forché. — 1st ed.
    p. cm.
  ISBN 0-06-017078-6
  I. Title.
  PS3556.068A83 1994
  811'.54—dc20   93-37208

94 95 96 97 98 ❖/RRD 10 9 8 7 6 5 4 3 2 1

"The Recording Angel" appeared in *Antaeus* and then in *The Best American Poetry of 1991*, edited by Mark Strand and David Lehman (New York: Collier Books, 1992). An early version of "The Notebook of Uprising" appeared in the Twentieth Anniversary Issue of *The American Poetry Review* in 1993. An early version of "The Angel of History" was published by *The Graham House Review* in a special issue dedicated to the memory of Terrence Des Pres. "Book Codes" appeared in *No Roses Review*. I wish to thank the National Endowment for the Arts and the Lannan Foundation for fellowships that enabled this work to be completed.

for Harry and Sean Christophe

This is how one pictures the angel of history. His face is turned toward the past. Where we perceive a chain of events, he sees one single catastrophe which keeps piling wreckage and hurls it in front of his feet. The angel would like to stay, awaken the dead, and make whole what has been smashed. But a storm is blowing in from Paradise; it has got caught in his wings with such a violence that the angel can no longer close them. The storm irresistibly propels him into the future to which his back is turned, while the pile of debris before him grows skyward.

—WALTER BENJAMIN, "Theses on the Philosophy of History," IX

Contents

PART I

The Angel of History

There are times when the child seems delicate, as if he had not yet crossed into the world.
When French was the secret music of the street, the café, the train, my own
                receded and became intimacy and sleep.
In the world it was the language of propaganda, the agreed-upon lie, and it bound me to
                itself, demanding of my life an explanation.
When my son was born I became mortal.

Our days at Cape Enrage, a bleached shack of rented rooms and white air. April.
At the low tide acres of light, boats abandoned by water.
While sleeping, the child vanishes from his life.

Years later, on the boat from Beirut, or before the boat, an hour before, helicopters lifting
                a white veil of sea.
A woman broken into many women.

These boats, forgotten, have no keels. So it is safe for them, and the emptiness beneath
    them safe.
April was here briefly. The breakwater visible, the lighthouse, but no horizon.
The music resembled April, the gulls, April, but you weren't walking toward this house.
If the child knew words, if it weren't necessary for him to question me with his hands—
To have known returning would be like this,
        that the sea light of April had been your vigilance.

———————————

In the night-vaulted corridors of the Hôtel-Dieu, a sleepless woman pushes her stretcher
    along the corridors of the past. *Bonjour, madame. Je m'appelle Ellie.*

There were trains, and beneath them, laddered fields.

Autumns the fields were deliberately burned by a fire so harmless children ran through it
    making up a sort of game.
Women beat the flames with brooms and blankets, so the fires were said to be *under
    control.*

As for the children, they were forbidden to ask about the years before they were born.
Yet they burned the fields, yet everything was said to be *under control*
        with the single phrase *death traffic.*

———————————

This is Izieu during the war, Izieu and the neighboring village of Bregnier-Cordon.
This is a farmhouse in Izieu.
Itself a quiet place of stone houses over the Rhône, where between Aprils, forty-four
    children were
        hidden successfully for a year in view of the mountains.
Until the fields were black and snow fell all night over the little plaque which does not
    mention
        that they were Jewish children hidden April to April in Izieu near Bregnier-
    Cordon.

Comment me vint l'écriture? Comme un duvet d'oiseau sur ma vitre, en hiver.
In every window a blank photograph of their internment.

Within the house, the silence of God. Forty-four bedrolls, forty-four metal cups.
And *the silence of God is God.*

In Pithiviers and Beaune-la-Rolande, in Les Milles, Les Tourelles, Moussac and Aubagne,
    the silence of God is God.

The children were taken to Poland.
The children were taken to Auschwitz in Poland
        singing *Vous n'aurez pas L'Alsace et la Lorraine.*
In a farmhouse still standing in Izieu, *le silence de Dieu est Dieu.*

———————————

In the night-vaulted corridors of the Hôtel-Dieu it is winter.
If a city, ruin, if an animal, hunger.
If a grave, anonymous.
If a century, this.

*Are the present hundred years a long time? But first see whether a hundred years can
be present.*

We lived in Ste. Monique ward over the main corridor, Ellie and myself, in the Hôtel-
  Dieu on the Place du Parvis Notre Dame.
Below us jonquils opened.
Ellie was afflicted with scales again, tiny Ellie, at the edge of her bed, peeling her skin
  from her arm as if it were an opera glove,
and weeping *cachée, cachée, cachée* all during the war.

Barn to barn in the haylight, field to cellar. Winter took one of her sons, and her own
  attempt to silence him, the other.

Le Dieu? Le Dieu est un feu.   A psychopath.   Le Dieu est feu.

It isn't normal for a mother to outlive her children.
It isn't normal that my sons should be dead.

Paris! Oh, how I loathe this city because of its past.

Then you wish to leave Paris?

Mais oui. I wish to leave life, *my dear.*
My parents? Deported. My aunts and uncles? Deported. My friends? All of them
  deportees.
I don't know what became of a single one. How they came to the end.
My papers said I was Polish. When the money ran out, we ran. When the Nazis came,
  we ran. Cachée, cachée, cachée!

The tubercular man offers his cigarette and the snow falls, patiently, across the spring
  flowers.

My life, triste. Do you understand? This place. No good! France. No good! Germany.
  No good! Ni l'Union soviétique. Fascists! It is no good.

Then why not leave Paris?

I am Jewish. Do you understand? Alone in a small room on the third floor, always alone.
To remain sane, I sing librettos to myself, and German lullabies, can you imagine?

Mein Flügel ist zum Schwung bereit
ich kehrte gern zurück,
denn bleib ich auch lebendige Zeit
ich hätte wenig Glück

My husband was a soldier against the Nazis.   Résistance. Agir.   He wasn't killed in
  the war.
He even returned to me. It was after the war he died. He died of cholera.
    And the world is worse now than it was then.

Worse?
Mais oui!

———————

We must wear our slippers and not smoke. We must not go further than the sign No
   ADMITTANCE.

*No — a little residue of nothing.   And admittance, what does it mean? That they are
        not going to blame themselves for anything.*
*But the deportees, no, there is nothing between the word and those who are not, who do not
        reviennent.*
And if language is an arbitrary system, one must not go further than the sign No
   ADMITTANCE
        in the Hôtel-Dieu on the Place du Parvis Notre Dame.

———————————

Then my husband came with our child in his arms and stood outside Ste. Monique.
    They would not permit the child near my bed.
A tuberculosis wing in winter.
You go out then in the hallway, yes. You have the right to see your child. Don't let
    anyone stop you. They are all fascists.

A rain through raised windows, as in: you must not forget anything: the hours, hope,
    sleeplessness,
    and the trains, you must not forgive them.
Smoke rising from the fields, the death of a husband, winter's
    breath and the moonlight that reached the pallet.
Hunger, and the knife of waking, the cold knife.

In April, the lilacs come, wrapped in *Le Monde.*

"A plane went down in Warsaw this afternoon."

There was time to imagine it: a wedding dress hanging in a toolshed outside Warsaw.

But when asked in what sense the world was worse, she answered *Pardon, est-ce que je vous dérange?*

Je ne sais pas très bien m'éxpliquer en français.

Hôtel-Dieu? Some people say so. I say this God is insane.

———————

We held roses, then the roses rested on the snow as if someone had died there. Winter.
  There were many
        graves. All the same kind.
So it would be a cemetery of war. . . .

They died and were buried in mud but their hands protruded.
      So their friends used the hands to hang helmets on.

And the fields? Aren't the fields changed by what happened?
      The dead aren't like us.
How can the fields continue as simple fields?

The child has gone to the city with his father. They are en route past remaining weeks
      of boarded summer houses, beach pine, a blue water tower.
The winter residents are packing for spring.
You should return to Ellie. You mustn't leave her alone.
But we've lost days, and many times tried to begin again, while she locks herself in the
    water closet to sing.
        (The words are somewhere. The words belong here.)
Her skin sloughing in the hard towels.
And just then the doves rise and batter the wind.

In my absence, the child took his first step alone,
      moving along the white hallway without help but at night nearly drowning in
    my own breath.
Ellie lifting tissues of herself from herself.
Here, in this book, I have found your illness. It is called St. Anthony's Fire.

I don't go out now. It's a terrible thing to see me walk.
      (The bell of her husband's ax breaking open the river.)

It is worse than memory, the open country of death.

———————————

A tall light entered the room. The windows, hand blown, were those of occupied Paris.
I was waiting for the child's birth.
There were cut tulips in the glass.

Simone was alive. Twice her hand reached to fold the blue shutters back over the
   windows, and once she
         touched the window as I passed.
Under the plane trees of Montparnasse:
         The cemetery workman's wheelbarrow, an old woman's knowledge of graves.

That first week after his birth were wet balconies and voile. White roses.
         And God's name *a boneless string of vowels.*

And just now it was as if someone not alive were watching,
          so I asked if he'd suffered very much and he said *no*.

But when I came back from the border something odd happened.
It had been more than seventy days and I weighed nothing.
My bags were no heavier than usual but I couldn't lift them.
After a drink and some talk I went for a rest.
When I woke my room was filled with vultures.
They were hopping about the room, belching and vomiting flesh,
          as you saw them at Puerto Diablo and El Playon.

Exactly as you saw them.

As if someone not alive were watching.
On the sill, the bureau, in the bath and on my body

So fat with flesh they weren't able to fly

And when I turned, there was nothing,
          as someone asks, Is something wrong?

———————

In the window of my earlier life, it is often winter, a glass white with my own breath,
     and in rubbing it clear I see only my own reflection.

It was years before my face would become hers, yours, and hers, the other's, facing
     each other through days, pain, the prisoner's visiting window.

Adjusting the light so as to see again, so as to commit memory to our features, my eyes,
     hers, our breath, hers, my own—

As if it were possible to go on living for someone else.

When she walked home with me, *for me*, toward the National Palace, then inside
     with me to prevent my going alone.

Knowing each would give the other her own life, I live yours now, the one you might
   have lived in Paris,
          and your daughters are with me.

We have festivals in memory of you, and nightmares in which you tell us

It is never night when you die.

Eight years later in France I opened your letter as if you had sent it years before we
   were parted.
            On blue foolscap in your own hand:

What has become of us? The factory work has aged me, threaded my hair with tin,
            buried my eyes in my face, taken a few of my teeth
            and emptied my body of its fruits.

My children have grown and live separate from me in exile. I haven't seen them, nor the
            children they've had.
The broken mountains have become neutral.

I have in my possession his diary, a sack of the clothing they cut from his body, the
   photograph taken
            before the war, and I call it the war now, I no longer call it the struggle.

Our house has fallen and the debris prevents me from digging up what we buried behind
   it many years ago.

Please, when you write, describe again how I looked in the white dress that improbable
   morning
            when my random life was caught in a net of purpose.

———————————

Here you live in an atelier beside Simone's overlooking the cemetery.
Here you are in exile but can't afford to buy a clock.
Here at café tables you write letters to the disappeared and, worse, mail them.
Here you taste *rascasse,* a fish you never will have tasted.
Here you open your arms when the man who might have loved you comes.

Surely all art is the result of one's having been in danger, of having gone through an
    experience all the way to the end.

As the last helicopter lifted away from the deck of the Manitowac and the ship turned

Bonsoir, madame. Je m'appelle Ellie.

A colander of starlight, the sky in that part of the world.

A wedding dress hanging in a toolshed outside Warsaw.

Bonsoir. Est-ce que je vous dérange?

On the contrary, I'm happy to practice speaking.

*Then you aren't French. How fortunate for me. I couldn't have shared this room with a
    French woman.*

While the white phosphorous bombs plumed into the air like ostrich feathers of light
    and I cursed you for
            remaining there without me, for tricking me into this departure.

Parlez-vous français? Est-ce que vous le parlez bien?

So beautiful, ma'am, from here, the sailor said, if you don't stop to think.

And it went on like that all night, questions in French, and it went on, radiant white
    feathers along the coast of Lebanon, until Ellie slept.

———————

How can one confuse that much destruction with one woman's painful life?

Est-ce que je vous dérange? she asked. *Et pourquoi des questions?*

Because in French there is no auxiliary verb corresponding to our English *did*

As in

Did you wait for him to come back? and Did he return from the war alive?

Or

Did you decide in Beirut to go on without him?

As if someone not alive were watching:
Bonsoir. Est-ce que je vous dérange?

Night terrors.   A city with all its windows blank.
A memory through which one hasn't lived.

You see, I told Madame about my life.
I told her everything.
And what did she say?

PART II

The Notebook of Uprising

"What will be is not; and what would be;
what was, what might have been, they are not."

—PAUL VALÉRY, *Parables*

I

The hand moves across the page of its own accord.
The first years are a yellow field, and a child singing through her crib bars.
Yours, the windblown canola between the curtain and hope. Mine, the languor of
      peony in a time unknown to us.
You wanted only to retrieve a few invisible souvenirs:
      words spoken by coals in a tile oven,
      empty iron benches wrapped in snow.

Anna said we were all to be sent: Poles, Romanians, Gypsies.
So she drew her finger across her throat.

II

Anna stands in a ring of thawed snow, stirring a trash fire in an iron drum until her face
        flares, shriveled and intent, and sparks rise in the night along with pages of
    burning
            ash from the week's papers,
            one peeling away from the rest,
an ashen page framed in brilliance.

For a moment, the words are visible, even though fire has destroyed them, so
        transparent has the page become.
The sparks from this fire hiss out among the stars and in thirty years appear
        as tracer rounds.

They didn't want you to know the past. They were hoping in this way you could escape it.

III

Smoke wrote from its fire something brief
      in the city of what could be said.
As if a cemetery were a field of doors. *Requia* crying against the walls. Little roofs of
   moonlight.
The ecstasy of standing outside oneself—

Anna said "carry this" and "follow behind me."
The earth is tired and marked, human after human.

IV

So we are going back, to the invisible railyard shed and the poppy-seed cakes.
Anna, coal-eyed in a field of bone chips.

When you were born a steamed pot lid was shaken over your face to provide tears for a
     lifetime.
          This is why you have such happiness no matter what.
Were these the animals of your village? Pigs, goats, geese, a few cows?

Pigs with their throats cut. Goats eating flowers. Crows descending on a child to pull
     hair for their nests.

You loved the shabbiness of the world: countries invaded, cities bombed, houses whose
     roofs have fallen in,
          women who have lost their men, orphans, amputees, the war wounded.
What you did not love any longer was a world that had lost its soul.

V

There are more geese than people in this village and the geese know it. They march
   through the streets
        kicking their feet high like the Germans and, later, the Russians.
On parade, necks craned, beaks open, honking like German jeeps and, later, Russian.

    I am not sure what the photograph has to do with what happened.

One went to sweep the schools clean in a mountain town. Another took his life but
   where did he take it?
Don't believe Western news reports: a carnival of resistance. Rather, think of it this way: you
    are an insomniac who has gone to bed on an ordinary August night.

VI

Alenka: *You must not speak anymore. I am going to tell you.*

VII

His grave is strewn with slipper flowers in a coppice of loss.
      The girl whose uncle was a violin, Borovská.
Years taken from them: birch light, his breath in her mouth, *what do we have to forget?*
      In 1941 he knew her, all shawl, her fear.
A basket of bread and *klobása* wrapped in pain.
      That he had escaped the fate of the others was unknown to her.

VIII

This is close, and passing time brings it no closer: the years, cities moving beside a train.

What comes back? That Matejka could fold his ears up and stick them inside his head.
That the women of his village pissed standing up.
All winter, sandwiches of duck fat.

Then someone calling. It might be from the past. It has that quality.

IX

Folded swans in the mirror, Vltava,
your hand on the bridge rail
in a blackened city under a soot heaven
holding a banner completely fashioned of hope.

X

Beyond the tarred Teplice road, past cut fields, tarpaulin-covered hayricks,
      petrochemical plants spewing black smoke,
Poppies afflicted the hayfields with wounding brilliance.

The people were harvesting cauliflower then from the gardens of Terezin.
Blank-eyed, a boy pedaled a bicycle back and forth with a naked broken doll in its basket.

At the prison gate a woman stood holding a bouquet of leeks wrapped in paper.
Two Czech soldiers strolled through what had once been the women's compound.
Doors opened and closed, swallows dipped into the prison yard and rose.
We walked the cold, swept-clean barracks, ran our hands down long trestle tables and
    tiered bunks.
We picked forget-me-nots and left them where he died.
Somewhere here, somewhere with his name carved into a wall, are the words
      into your sun-blessed life.

XI

In the café across from Zivnostenská banka we are able to buy
      a sack of bread for the road, and poppies.
In the tin light we walk, our sandwiches in foil
      like the light along Národní, street of the kiosks.

The wind has eaten the faces from the angels of Charles Bridge
      as if the earth were finished with us.

We leave our *konvalinka* for the saint, white tulips for the mother of God.

XII

Along Leninova, soot pines and state trucks,
          a world emptying of human belief.

Since the war, they begin, or *after the invasion:*
a little stiff bread to soak up the blood
(meat and boiled potatoes),
a small silence for each of them,
salt in the palm,
a cold stone of bitterness.

"It is playing chess with us."

XIII

A two-hour queue for pears, a waxen hill of spent tapers where
        Jan Palach immolated himself.
Meat lines, bridge lights in the Vltava.

In a child's leather prayer book from Terezin: V.K. 1940, hearts, a police doll wearing
    the star.

This is Hana Minka's field of flowers.
This is Gabi Friová's imaginary house.

There are flowers growing on the roofs of the cell blocks, the low bricked grass-roofed
    prisons,
        the *au revoir* of the tunnels.

In starvation rooms along a wall of fading blue figures
        a fresco of hair the blue of bread smoke.

On a wreath's black ribbon, the word for scaffold: *popraviště.*

XIV

We cross the Danube into a world in decline:
     nothing has changed here, nothing is as it was.

Darkening lindens, drunks beneath sodium lamps, the bottles belling against the cobbles.

On the back page of a calendar, 1938: ". . . to the courthouse to be taken away."
The word on the empty box: *Important*   (all the boxes empty).

In the leather valise, a Dominican habit, altar linens, soap, the clothing of a railway
     conductor wrapped in *Rudé Právo*
Moth-winged curtains, a blizzard of moths from a trunk's maw, piano and corpse dust,
     gold attic shafts of spirit.

In the diary ". . . whoever it was went to prison,"
     a window not opened in twenty-two years.

XV

The past is not where you left it, Svetko.
It is a ruined city, spackled with grief,
      The house, still yellow stucco with pear trees.
Empty swallow nests hang in the eaves
      woven with bits of collar and sleeve.
There is a diary open to the words *cannot remain here.*

XVI

What has eaten these walls? wind in the mustard fields.
Death maps.
Rat teeth.

Hurrying we find German war maps of the High Tatras where Anna lived, and one of
  Brno
        as if there were a corpse in the armoire.

XVII

A mirror of swans, a gesture of regret, bridge stones rippling in the Vltava,
       your face strewn with childhood:

We were looking for _____ we found _____.

The hourly figures struck each other.
They knew the time was passing in which we are now suspended.

As long as it takes snow to slip from the coal piles,
       a memory barely retrieved from a fire is (the past) in its hiding place.

XVIII

We find her in a block of worker housing flats on a small *náměstí* bordering a ditch
        near one of the places where
Hitler could have been stopped.

Her name appears in a column of names: *Borovská.*

My voice fills the call box:
"This is the granddaughter of Anna Bassarová and the daughter of Michal."

There was so much weeping, she said, but never anyone.
A language even paper would refuse,
bell music rolling down the cold roofs,
their footsteps disappearing as they walked.

She stood on the landing of disbelief in Brno as if the war were translucent behind us,
        the little ones in graves the size of pillows.

XIX

This is a map drawn from memory of the specular itinerary of exile.

An erasure of everything destroyed yet left intact:

Nuit blanche, your nights awake and the white window winter-locked.

Kafka drawn in soft coal.

If we died we might escape the sovereignty of the accidental:

　　　　hours on line to fill a basket of provisions in the open-air cathedral of Prague,

as one who, keeping still, announces herself

the other night where, precisely . . .

from the village of the first person,

in a time no longer remote.

Before enduring it we will endure it.

XX

This is what we have taken the ordinary world to mean:
bootprints in clay,
the persistence of tracked field.

What was here before imperfectly erased
        and memory a reliquary in a wall of silence.

XXI

Near the stone walls of the bridgeworks we met night after night but no one knew it.
Poppies and cinquefoil, an empty concrete flood pit.

      Grapes ripening in fog.

It is only today that he has disappeared altogether.
The memories are few and like dreams of her life resuming a muted sound of snow
    falling into itself.

In the photograph holding each other with the attention wind gives the fields.
With a field's sense of shovels.

The bruise, his broken words, and those who wait for him.

It will be winter then, winter, before we see him again.
Not this winter but another.

XXII

A little burnt sorrow, truck-rutted fields—
        that someone attempted to hide this is evidence enough.
In the wounded kitchen, Borovská begins:
Put into question others, put into question God.
Whatever can be taken away is taken
to allow suffering to remain.

Autumn. That autumn. Other autumns.
It was as if we'd been given to walk through a world to come.

XXIII

In a small hotel built not on its own remains but in place of itself:
Stiff bread and blue milk near the hissing fire.
The child asleep in a box by the stove.
A woman's face in lamplight, a misted woman blurring herself with soap in a stall shower.
A man whose name she doesn't ask is given a bed and she watches him take sleep and
        through the split curtain studies the street.
Lifting a tiny corner of tissue from the window to the glassy weather of March:
        it is still there, damaged yellow paper.
The train rose along the bank above the tiled roofs, its windows blinded by mud and
    smoke.

XXIV

The same bells ringing then.
Flutes of wind through bullet holes and the sky pitch-smoke.

(She would have hidden her) the woman in whom she hides herself. . . .

An ash tree in the yard fifty years, soft-barked and bare-leafed as when
        she peeled the blackout paper from the casement
for a glimpse of the hushed gray world of a war without end.

So she stood with her hopes at sail among linens and slept through her childhood in his
    arms
        more actually than if she'd been with him.

XXV

East Berlin is swept clean, its walks sheltered by oaks. There is nothing to buy. People
        stroll and talk, they queue at bookstores.
No one knows where Brecht is buried or where Benjamin lived.

Wie im himmel so auf erden as in heaven so on earth.
Wer ist unser gott? who is our god?

A sign behind the black-windowed Reichstag reads "these are the last days."

Breaking holes in the wall, they found nothing.
The homeless squatters passed through the holes into empty communist gardens,
        and the people from the east passed from their side
        into a world unbearable to them.

XXVI

Storm light, bare orchards, the heavens briefly open.
My heart flew to his roof.

We returned here after the war whose lives the war took.

Last summer a wind from Byelorussia brought us blue roses.

Something was wrong with the milk.
Yellow brooks of waste lit the hayfields.

XXVII

If you ask them anything they go on telling you the same thing forever.
Not what happened, but what may happen.
Death understood as death.
The world in its worlding.
Our hope put into question.
Figures dead and alive
         whispering not truth but a need for truth when one word is many things.

XXVIII

They've made a shrine in hissing rain to Jan Palach near where four men are starving
    themselves to death.
These are the zones of refuse: that dream, and the train taking us,
        a bell ringing in my spine.

Every epoch bears its own ending within itself.
Fields of rape, canola fields, the white-eyed, walking dead.

So the cry is cut from its stalk.

PART III

The Recording Angel

I

Memory insists she stood there, able to go neither forward nor back, and in that
Unanimous night, time slowed, in light pulsing through ash, light of which the coat was
    made
Light of their brick houses
In matter's choreography of light, time slowed, then reversed until memory
Held her, able to go neither forward nor back
They were alone where once hundreds of thousands lived

Doves, or rather their wings, heard above the roof and the linens floating
Above a comic wedding in which corpses exchange vows. A grand funeral celebration
Everyone has died at once
Walking home always, always on this same blue road, cold through the black-and-white
    trees
Unless the film were reversed, she wouldn't reach the house
As she doesn't in her memory, or in her dream
Often she hears him calling out, half her name, his own, behind her in a room until she
    turns
Standing forever, where often she hears him calling out

He is there, hidden in the blue winter fields and the burnt acreage of summer
As if, in reflecting the ruins, the river were filming what their city had been
And *had it not been for this* lines up behind *if it weren't for that*
Until the past is something of a regiment
Yet looking back down the row of marching faces one sees one face
Before the shelling, these balconies were for geraniums and children
The slate roofs for morning

Market flowers in a jar, a string of tied garlic, and a voice moving off as if fearing itself
Under the leprous trees a white siren of light searches
Under the leprous trees a white siren of sun

II

A row of cabanas with white towels near restorative waters where once it was possible
    to be cured
A town of vacant summer houses
Mists burning the slightest lapse of sea
The child has gone to the window filled with desire, a glass light passing through its hand
There are tide tables by which the sea had been predictable, as were the heavens
As sickness chose from among us we grew fewer
There were jetty lights where there was no jetty
What the rain forests had been became our difficult breath

At the moment when the snow geese lifted, thousands at once after days of crying in
    the wetlands
At once they lifted in a single ascent, acres of wind in their wingbones
Wetlands of morning light in their lift moving as one over the continent
As a white front, one in their radiance, in their crying, a cloud of one desire

The child plays with its dead telephone. The father blows a kiss. The child laughs
The fire of his few years is carried toward the child on a cake
The child can't help itself. Would each day be like this?

And the geese, rising and falling in the rain on a surf of black hands
Sheets of rain and geese invisible or gone

Someone was supposed to have come
Waves turning black with the beach weed called dead men's hands
The sea strikes a bottle against a rock

III

The photographs were found at first by mistake in the drawer. After that I went to
    them often
She was standing on her toes in a silk *yukata*, her arms raised
Wearing a girl's white socks and near her feet a vase of calla lilies
Otherwise she wore nothing
And in this one, her long hair is gathered into a white towel
Or tied back not to interfere
She had been wounded by so many men, abused by them
From behind in a silk *yukata*, then like this
One morning they were gone and I searched his belongings for them like a madwoman
In every direction, melted railyards, felled telegraph poles
For two months to find some trace of her
Footsteps on the floor above. More birds
It might have been less painful had it not been for the photographs
And beyond the paper walls, the red maple
Shirt in the wind of what the past meant
The fresh claw of a swastika on Rue Boulard
A man walking until he can no longer be seen
Don't say I was there. Always say I was never there.

IV

The child asks about earth
The earth is a school. It is a waiting room, a foyer giving onto emptiness
It is for desires, small but beautifully done
The earth is wrapped in weather, and the weather in risen words
The child is awake, singing to himself, speaking in a language ending with the word *night*
Unaware of the sea entering, of the eternal dunes burying
Wooden matchsticks in a cup
The meaning of an object or its lack
Their preoccupation with suitcases and their contents
God returns to the world from within and the past
Is circular, like consequence
The earth tentative, blue: a fire wrapped in cold water
A sudden gust of yellow tickets, a cold blue rail and some boat lights
The barrier dunes, blue asters, the parabolic dunes, and wind
The children have returned to the beach, this time a boy and a girl
Hurrying toward then away from the water
He is wearing a red jacket and it is not important, the jacket
The child asks if fish have tongues. The other laughs, giving white tissues to the dog
A white sail tied over the bay's mouth muffles the sea
On the water's map, little x's: a cross-stitched sampler of cries for help
And yet every lost one has been seen, mornings in winter, and at night
When the fishermen have cast their nets one too many times
They surface, the lost, drawing great hillocks of breath
We on the shore no longer vanish when the beacon strokes us
The child's boat plies the water in imitation of boats
Years they sought her, whose crew left on the water a sad Welsh hymn
Voices from a ketch lit by candles
Days pass and nothing occurs, nights pass, nights, and life continues in its passing
We must try then to send a message ending with the word *night*

V

A river that later caught fire
A stone with its own list of names
Nothing that worked once can be tried again
That's what he told me. I didn't know. I worked as a housewife then, bound to the
     passing meals
The need for linens, the demand to return flying clothes to their hooks.
At night I found myself in a pasture of refuse
After the city vanished, they were carried on black mats from one place
To another with no one to answer them
Vultures watching from the white trees
A portable safe found stuffed with charred paper
An incense burner fused to its black prayer
In the city's perfect emanation of light
We lost every alternate route
We were there, ill there, in the new birthplace of humanity

In the last of the world's open cities, rain begins
The china cups are cleared from the chiming tables
A garden of black silk blooms
Forget the fish, the bottle, the bath towels stiffening on the grate
Sleeveless pajamas, skirts of fire and flowers
A girl's face turned toward a cup of water with no mouth
Hello child, hang your coat here. This is what she said after so many years. This was all
     she said

VI

Then they all got drunk
Sylvia continued to mourn her brother
Madame please? A bit of newspaper. I would like to relieve myself
He sings to the work-for-nothings, the die-laughing of hungers
As if his voice could grow pumpkins out of the white ground
Even the sign warning us away implied an obligation to go on
A bottle, a red bandanna, a yellow bucket of bones behind the gate
We find a shovel near all of this
And as these were the final months, a radio

It was an island wrapped in white fog, Angel Island, a wingless rock, a way station
Now it isn't possible to go further, paper thin and floating
Each small act of defiance a force
There would be blank winds in the debris and palm carnage in the half-life
Our faces are there
Mine bears the mark of your palm, yours the marks of gelignite
A bar of light touches the floor of a house long since torn down
Where the walls were, silence was
The playing cards you clipped to a window fan
To imitate the sound of helicopters all those nights
So as to return to the ruins of a wished-for life

Their flesh like fallen snow
Leaf shadows burnt into a post
Burns of bamboo on bamboo canes
These ruins are to the future what the past is to us

VII

Someone has written fuck with dogshit on the walls of Simone's atelier
A pall of exhaust over Paris
The woman with the shaved head seen twice in different arrondissements
And on the Rue Victor Considerant, a boy with a white toy M-16
The days marched shouldering their little events
Tiny birds on the dining tables flew from spoon to bowl
As far as anyone knew, no one drowned
The hotel is no longer there
We were its final guests
A stone wall, white roses, birds and the whine of bright aerial antennas
Every window casement an empty portrait: radiant, formless, ancestral
In which he longs for her, whomever, her white bed
The remote possibility of another life
To look in the windows of that little place expecting someone
The two of us, the child, the two blue boats and the brown
The child comes into the room and leaves, comes and leaves

I loved her, he said, she was the woman of my life. Her blank eyes, her _____
This is what he loved
She sliced the photographs from their frames, chose what to bring with us, said
"Look what they've done to the windows! To my life."

You are a child, you think only of love, in whose other arms you will find refuge
The man walks on, blank and without veering
Where there are objects, he walks over rather than around them
The knife rises in her hand as she wipes her eyes
Comment vivre sans inconnu devant soi?
He departed with great pledges of love and went back to his life never to call her again

VIII

Dear L, I thought I knew what I was doing
On the island, a fuselage of wrecked plane, a wing in sharp vegetation
A radar dish filled with pumpkin plants
The blue wash of a cratered road
One thinks: the way back under cover of darkness with sufficient rounds
As sickness chose from among us, we grew fewer
And so as not to appear in uniform he walked in his underwear
Through the village as if he were only strolling the asylum grounds

One morning slides aqua into the next, the night beach lit and tired
Grève painted on the wall but what *Grève?* Nothing to strike for here. Better pay?
Better pay for what? Everybody in this no-name village is *chômeur*
It means they would carry your shit for you from your ass to the pit if they were paid
They plant flowers in cracker cans on the porch stair. They plant hibiscus in their
    wrecked cars
When you are talking about stupidity, only the military knows the meaning of the
    word *infinite*

Always he travels without maps as it is better to become lost than spend time thinking
    about the road
He drinks holy water, then pours some into a bottle in case he needs it again
Sometimes he uses vodka for the same end
Perhaps you have seen one of them?
A familiar man or woman, maimed, or a beggar who appears in several places at once

Why now and in such numbers?
If there are two doors, then only one gives onto normal life
Here, in this open field, that can never be a field again

IX

It isn't necessary to explain
The dead girl was thought to be with child
Until it was discovered that her belly had already been cut open
And a man's head placed where the child would have been
The tanks dug ladders in the earth no one was able to climb
In every war someone puts a cigarette in the corpse's mouth
And the corpse
The corpse is never mentioned
In the hours before his empty body was found
It was this, this life that he longed for, this that he wrote of desiring,
Yet this life leaves out everything for which he lived

Hundreds of small clay heads discovered while planting coffee
A telescope through which it was possible to watch a fly crawling the neighbor's roof tiles
The last-minute journey to the border for no reason, the secret house where sports
    trophies were kept
That weren't sports trophies
Someone is trying to kill me, he said. He was always saying this
Oranges turning to glass on the trees, a field strewn with them
In his knapsack a bar of soap, a towel the size of a dinner napkin
A map of the world he has not opened that will one day correspond to the world he has
    seen

In the spring, lilacs and mud roads, and later blossoming wind
Then the drone of beetles in high grass as if the grass were droning
He said a tongue doesn't have bones
He said tit for tat
Like a sack filled then emptied then filled
He was thin, yes, but when he walked past it was not as if a human being had passed
And always he thought: this is it, the end of the world. God is coming

You were first in my thoughts, a chimera, first
Then in the whisper of a sack's progress over the earth you were speaking:
We doubt we exist. We doubt with certain wisdom the world
Such pains as you took to convert a bedroom into a fire base
Where an angry God, spilled blood itself, lives

X

Having taken these white rooms for a season, I imagine that it might be possible to recover
For an hour each afternoon I vow to sit in meditative expectancy
The light far on the rock promontory reaches Paris
Where an old man's hand reaches out of the Seine
His wristwatch brilliant enough to catch the eye of a boat captain
There are times when the child seems not yet to have crossed into the world
Despite having entered a body
Memory a wind passing through the blood trees within us
Someone was supposed to have come
He wrote: I tore open your letter and licked the envelope's seal for any lingering trace of
    you

In the worst of centuries, a merely difficult week, nothing, nothing, then from nothing,
    something
I noticed it today while walking to the pharmacy, where they were already selling
    woolen underwear
The market was closed. There were dead flowers for sale, dead marigolds, hydrangea,
    peony
Smoke rose in a perfect line from the roof
Then it wasn't possible to go further
Everything seemed intentionally placed where it was, even the garbage bins
The children marched, holding their booklets
Peach leaves slipped earthward. Wind filled with souvenir shops
Doves painted white on the stopped wind
Making up a sort of game

Lamps in fog. Light fingering the canals
And now the defenselessness for which there is no cure
But it is a matter of shared history, or, as it were, we lived the same lie
Why lie? Why not life, as you intended?
I have the memory of a child in the southern slums, lifting the lid of an abandoned toilet
The child on my back, how ever was it kept from singing?
And falling back toward night

It was as if someone not alive were watching
Slowly, that is, over time, itself a barrier
And just then the doves rose and battered the wind
Where a notebook was kept once during a visit
This is my cap. This is my coat. Here's my shaving gear in its linen sack.

PART IV

Elegy

The page opens to snow on a field: boot-holed month, black hour
the bottle in your coat half vodka half winter light.
To what and to whom does one say *yes*?
If God were the uncertain, would you cling to him?

Beneath a tattoo of stars the gate opens, so silent so like a tomb.
This is the city you most loved, an empty stairwell
where the next rain lifts invisibly from the Seine.

With solitude, your coat open, you walk
steadily as if the railings were there and your hands weren't passing through them.

"When things were ready, they poured on fuel and touched off the fire.
They waited for a high wind. It was very fine, that powdered bone.
It was put into sacks, and when there were enough we went to a bridge on the Narew
  River."

And even less explicit phrases survived:
"To make charcoal.
For laundry irons."
And so we revolt against silence with a bit of speaking.
The page is a charred field where the dead would have written
We went on. And it was like living through something again one could not live through
  again.

The soul behind you no longer inhabits your life: the unlit house
with its breathless windows and a chimney of ruined wings
where wind becomes an aria, your name, voices from a field,
And you, smoke, dissonance, a psalm, a stairwell.

The Garden Shukkei-en

By way of a vanished bridge we cross this river
as a cloud of lifted snow would ascend a mountain.

She has always been afraid to come here.

It is the river she most
remembers, the living
and the dead both crying for help.

A world that allowed neither tears nor lamentation.

The *matsu* trees brush her hair as she passes
beneath them, as do the shining strands of barbed wire.

Where this lake is, there was a lake,
where these black pine grow, there grew black pine.

Where there is no teahouse I see a wooden teahouse
and the corpses of those who slept in it.

On the opposite bank of the Ota, a weeping willow
etches its memory of their faces into the water.

Where light touches the face, the character for heart is written.

She strokes a burnt trunk wrapped in straw:
I was weak and my skin hung from my fingertips like cloth

Do you think for a moment we were human beings to them?

She comes to the stone angel holding paper cranes.
Not an angel, but a woman where she once had been,

who walks through the garden Shukkei-en
calling the carp to the surface by clapping her hands.

Do Americans think of us?

So she began as we squatted over the toilets:
If you want, I'll tell you, but nothing I say will be enough.

We tried to dress our burns with vegetable oil.

Her hair is the white froth of rice rising up kettlesides, her mind also.
In the postwar years she thought deeply about how to live.

The common greeting *dozo-yiroshku* is please take care of me.
All *hibakusha* still alive were children then.

A cemetery seen from the air is a child's city.

I don't like this particular red flower because
it reminds me of a woman's brain crushed under a roof.

Perhaps my language is too precise, and therefore difficult to understand?

We have not, all these years, felt what you call happiness.
But at times, with good fortune, we experience something close.
As our life resembles life, and this garden the garden.
And in the silence surrounding what happened to us

it is the bell to awaken God that we've heard ringing.

The Testimony of Light

Our life is a fire dampened, or a fire shut up in stone.

—JACOB BOEHME, *De Incarnatione Verbi*

Outside everything visible and invisible a blazing maple.
Daybreak: a seam at the curve of the world.   The trousered legs of the women
   shimmered.
They held their arms in front of them like ghosts.

The coal bones of the house clinked in a kimono of smoke.
An attention hovered over the dream where the world had been.

For if Hiroshima in the morning, after the bomb has fallen,
    is like a dream, one must ask whose dream it is.

Must understand how not to speak would carry it with us.
With bones put into rice bowls.
While the baby crawled over its dead mother seeking milk.

Muga-muchu: without self, without center. Thrown up in the sky by a wind.

The way back is lost, the one obsession.
The worst is over.
The worst is yet to come.

PART V

Book Codes: I

We must know *whether*
And if not: then what is the task
very much on the surface
by means of finite signs
when one is frightened of the truth
"Are there simple things?"
   What depends on my life?
would be possible for me to write
like the film on deep water
over too wide chasms of thought
the world does not change
the visual field has not a form like this
so many graces of fate
the boundary (not a part) of the world
mirrored in its use
nothing except what can be said

Book Codes: II

a field tunneled by mice the same thought continually
like two hands indissolubly clasped to begin
as if in a coffin and can therefore think of nothing else
how incomplete a moment is human life

fragments together into a story before the shape of the whole
like a madman—time and again torn from my mouth
out of a nearby chimney each child's hand was taken
though this is not a fairy tale explained in advance

the sign of the cross on an invisible face with the calm of a butcher
as if it bore witness to some truth
with whom every connection had been severed
as if in a coffin and can therefore think of nothing else

an afternoon swallowing down whole years its every hour
troops marching by in the snow until they are transparent
from the woods through tall firs a wood with no apparent end
cathedrals at the tip of our tongues with countries not yet seen

whoever can cry should come here

Book Codes: III

stories no more substantial than the clouds or what had been his face
the view, the wind, the light disposing of the bodies
who walked in the realm of dreams but like everything else

for our having tried to cross the river caught between walls
one could hear a voice "Bear the unbearable"
and the broadcast was at an end

you might relay the message the rivers and mountains remained
the unseen figure of the enemy entirely covered
the central portion of their visual fields this blindness for names

the bone became black with flies again hatching in ruins
here were the black, burnt ceilings and boxes of flags
the walls covered with soot like a kitchen

smaller clouds spread out a golden screen
given the task of painting wounds
through the darkened town as though it had been light

at the moment of the birth of this cloud

The angel handed me a book, saying, "It contains everything that you could possibly wish to know." And he disappeared.

So I opened the book, which was not particularly fat.

It was written in an unknown character.

Scholars translated it, but they produced altogether different versions.

They differed even about the very senses of their own readings, agreeing upon neither the tops nor the bottoms of them, nor upon the beginnings of them nor the ends.

Toward the close of this vision it seemed to me that the book melted, until it could no longer be distinguished from this world that is about us.

—Paul Valéry

I would like to express my gratitude to
the closest reader of this work, Henry Mattison,
and also to Svetozár Daniel Simko, Honor Moore, and C. D. Wright.

Notes

The Angel of History is not about experiences. It is for me the opening of a wound, the muffling and silence of a decade, and it is also a gathering of utterances that have lifted away from the earth and wrapped it in a weather of risen words. These utterances issue from my own encounter with the events of this century but do not represent "it." The first-person, free-verse, lyric-narrative poem of my earlier years has given way to a work which has desired its own bodying forth: polyphonic, broken, haunted, and in ruins, with no possibility of restoration.

The epigraph is from Walter Benjamin's "Theses on the Philosophy of History," Part IX, from "Illuminations" by Walter Benjamin. Edited and with an introduction by Hannah Arendt.

"THE ANGEL OF HISTORY"

Hôtel-Dieu is a hospital near Notre Dame cathedral in Paris.
Comment me vint l'écriture . . . is from René Char's poem "La bibliothèque est en feu."
    Tr.: "How did writing come to me? As goose-down on my window in winter."
le silence de Dieu est Dieu is from Elie Weisel's poem "Ani Maamin."
Mein Flügel ist zum Schwung . . . is from Gershom Scholem's "Gruss vom Angelus,"
    included in Part IX of Walter Benjamin's "Theses on the Philosophy of History." Tr.:
    "My wing is ready for flight / I would like to turn back. / If I stayed timeless time, / I
    would have little luck."
a boneless string of vowels is from C. W. King, "Gnostics and Their Remains."
Puerto Diablo and El Playon were "body dumps" in El Salvador, where the remains of
    the "disappeared" were often left.

Passages arising out of El Salvador are dedicated to my husband, Harry Mattison, and my friend Margarita Herrera.

"THE NOTEBOOK OF UPRISINGS"

Anna refers to my paternal grandmother, Anna Bassarová.

Part IV derives from a tribute to the French photographer, Henri Cartier-Bresson.

Borovská is the surname of Zuzana Borovská, the daughter of my grandmother's sister. She lives in Brno, the capital of Moravia, which is now in the Czech Republic.

Vltava is the river that passes through Prague.

Teplice is a town on the road to Terezin.

Terezin is a town in the Czech Republic (formerly Czechoslovakia), where the Nazis located a prison and transit camp, Terezinstadt.

into your sun-blessed life is my translation of *dans ta vie ensoleillée*, a line from the poetry of Robert Desnos, who died at Terezinstadt, two days after the camp was liberated by Russian troops.

Živnostenská banka is a bank in Prague.

Národní is a street in Prague, where there are kiosks for news postings.

konvalinka is lily of the valley, which blooms in May and is sold in small bouquets on the streets of Prague.

Jan Palach is the young student who immolated himself in 1968 in protest of the Soviet and Warsaw Pact invasion of Czechoslovakia.

Hana Minka and Gabi Friová were children interned at Terezin.

Rudé Právo was the official Communist Party newspaper of Czechoslo-vakia.

Svetko refers to Svetozár Daniel Simko, the Czechoslovak-born American poet who left Czechoslovakia in 1969, following the Warsaw Pact invasion of his country.

náměstí: "square."

Nuit blanche (Fr.), "white night," refers to insomnia.

"a wind from Byelorussia" refers to the fallout-contaminated wind from the Chernobyl nuclear accident.

The world in its worlding is from Martin Heidegger.

"THE RECORDING ANGEL"

yukata is a Japanese robe, a shorter version of the *kimono*.

Don't say I was there. Always say I was never there is from Elias Canetti.

"At night I found myself in a pasture of refuse" is a *misprision* of Georg Trakl's *Nachts fand ich mich auf einer Heide, / Starrend von Unrat und Staub der Sterne*, from the poem "De Profundis." Daniel Simko's translation reads: "At night I found myself in a pasture, / Rigid with refuse and the dust of stars."

Simone refers to Simone de Beauvoir.

Comment vivre sans inconnu devant soi? is from René Char's poem "Argument," included in *Poems of René Char*, translated and annotated by Mary Ann Caws and Jonathan Griffin. Tr.: "How can we live without the unknown before us?"

Grève (Fr.): "strike."

chômeur (Fr.): "unemployed."

Where an angry God . . . is from Georg Trakl's poem "Grodek," included in "Autumn Sonata" by Georg Trakl, translated by Daniel Simko. Original: "*Rotes Gewölk, darin ein zürnender Gott wohnt.*"

This is my cap . . . is from Günter Eich's poem "Inventory," translated by Stuart Freibert, David Walker, and David Young, in *Valuable Nail. Günter Eich: Selected Poems.*

I am grateful to James Tate for helping this poem into the world.

"ELEGY"

"If God were the *uncertain,* would you cling to him?" is from Paul Valéry's "The Art of Poetry."

"When things were ready . . . wind" is from Motke Zaidl and Itzhak Dugin's description of Sobibor in Claude Lanzmann's film *Shoah.*

"It was very fine . . . Narew River" is an adaptation of Simon Srebnik's testimony on Chelmno in Lanzmann's film.

"To make charcoal . . . irons" was the answer given by an SS man to Simon Srebnik when he asked the purpose of the ovens at Chelmno, as stated in Lanzmann's film.

This poem is dedicated to the memory of Terrence Des Pres.

"THE GARDEN SHUKKEI-EN"

Shukkei-en is an ornamental garden in Hiroshima. It has been restored.

The Ota is one of the rivers of Hiroshima.